Above The Clouds: 100 Daily Devotions For Flight Attendants

by Dr. Melissa Weathersby

Apostle | Prophet | Author | Founder, Write This Way Publishing Incorporated

Write This Way Publishing Incorporated
www.WriteThisWay.Info
Printed in the United States of America

DEDICATION

This devotional is dedicated to every Kingdom builder, visionary, and believer who refuses to settle for less than God's best.

To Jesus Christ, the Author and Finisher of my faith, may every page point back to You.
To those walking through the refining fire, may these words remind you that process precedes power and that your pain is producing purpose.

To every writer, preacher, leader, and intercessor who still believes that obedience unlocks overflow. This is for you. Keep standing, keep speaking, and keep building even when no one claps, because Heaven is watching and your faith is being recorded in eternity.

And finally to the next generation of Prophets, Apostles, and Dreamers, may you rise with clarity, creativity, and conviction. The pen in your hand is not ordinary; it is an instrument of destiny.

Apostle Dr. Melissa Weathersby
Apostle Dr. Melissa Weathersby

Above The Clouds: 100 Daily Devotions For Flight Attendants

COPYRIGHT NOTICES

Copyright © 2025 Write This Way Publishing Incorporated
All rights reserved.

No part of this publication may be reproduced, distributed, or transmitted in any form or by any means—including photocopying, recording, or other electronic or mechanical methods—without the prior written permission of the publisher, except in the case of brief quotations used in reviews or certain noncommercial uses permitted by copyright law.

For permission requests, please contact:
Info@WriteThisWay.Info

Publisher:
Write This Way Publishing Incorporated

First Edition, 2025
Printed in the United States of America

ISBN: 978-1-7345994-5-9

Scripture Quotations:
Scripture quotations are taken from the [insert Bible translation name — e.g., New International Version® (NIV)]. Used by permission. All rights reserved worldwide.
Scripture accessed via BibleGateway.com.

If multiple translations were used, include:
Scripture quotations marked (NIV) are taken from The Holy Bible, New International Version®, NIV®.

Above The Clouds: 100 Daily Devotions For Flight Attendants

Copyright © 1973, 1978, 1984, 2011 by Biblica, Inc.™ Used by permission. All rights reserved worldwide.
Scripture quotations marked (KJV) are from the King James Version. Public domain.
Scripture quotations marked (NLT) are taken from the Holy Bible, New Living Translation, copyright © 1996, 2004, 2015 by Tyndale House Foundation. Used by permission of Tyndale House Publishers.

Disclaimer and Limitation of Liability:
The author and publisher have made every effort to ensure the accuracy of the information presented herein. However, they make no representations or warranties with respect to the completeness or applicability of the contents. The information is provided "as is" without warranty, express or implied. Neither the author nor the publisher shall be liable for any loss of profit, or any other commercial damages, including but not limited to special, incidental, consequential, or other damages.

The insights, prayers, and reflections contained in this devotional are designed for spiritual encouragement and personal growth. They are not intended to replace pastoral counseling, professional therapy, or financial advice where applicable. Seek the Lord for confirmation and personal direction as you apply these teachings to your own journey of faith.

Cover Design Assistance:
Cover concept and layout elements were developed with the assistance of ChatGPT, an AI tool by OpenAI, used strictly for design inspiration. All writing, editing, and final creative direction are the sole work and property of the author and Write This Way Publishing Incorporated.

Above The Clouds: 100 Daily Devotions For Flight Attendants

Published by:
Write This Way Publishing Incorporated
Info@WriteThisWay.Info | www.WriteThisWay.Info

ACKNOWLEDGMENTS

First and foremost, I give all glory and honor to God Almighty, whose wisdom, grace, and unfailing love guided every word of this devotional. Every revelation and reflection contained herein was birthed through prayer, obedience, and time in His presence. Without Him, there would be no purpose, no power, and no pages worth printing.

To my readers, thank you for allowing me to speak into your spiritual journey. I pray this devotional strengthens your faith, renews your vision, and draws you deeper into divine intimacy with the Father.

To my publishing family, Write This Way Publishing Incorporated, thank you for being the vehicle through which God's messages find their voice in the world. We are more than a publishing house; we are a movement of purpose and prophetic influence.

A special acknowledgment to ChatGPT by OpenAI, an AI language tool that provided creative design and formatting assistance in bringing this project to life. Technology served as a tool, but the anointing and authorship belong fully to the Lord.

Finally, to every believer, leader, and visionary who continues to write, speak, and live their faith with boldness. Keep building. Keep believing. Keep writing your way to purpose and prosperity.

With Kingdom love and prophetic vision,

Apostle Dr. Melissa Weathersby
Apostle Dr. Melissa Weathersby
Founder, Write This Way Publishing Incorporated

ABOUT THE AUTHOR

Dr. Melissa Weathersby
Financial Wellness Strategist | Educator | Author | Keynote Speaker | Apostle

Dr. Melissa Weathersby is a powerhouse in the intersecting worlds of financial wellness, higher education, leadership, and faith. A published author, certified financial educator, ordained Apostle, Prophet, and Pastor and seasoned keynote speaker, she brings over two decades of experience in equipping individuals and institutions to thrive- financially, professionally, and spiritually.

As a Certified Financial Education Instructor (CFEI®) and a member of the Forbes Coaches Council, Dr. Weathersby is a recognized voice in national conversations around financial literacy and leadership. She has spoken at major conferences such as the National Institute for Staff and Organizational Development and Texas State University's Leadership Institute and has been featured as an expert panelist on TAAN TV, Oasis Fellowship Church, and more. Her impact spans both the corporate and faith-based worlds, with an emphasis on empowerment through practical strategies, biblical insight, and real-world financial principles. She has ignited platforms such as TBN's Praise the Lord show and Bishop T.D. Jake's Megafest event.

Dr. Weathersby holds a Doctorate in Education (Adult Learning and Higher Education) and is the author of multiple books, including *Money Medic: Financial Solutions During Times of Crisis*, *Write This Way Workbook*, and *How to Get Approved for a Mortgage... the First Time.* She has also authored several Texas Real Estate Commission-approved textbooks. Her thought leadership is featured across numerous Forbes articles addressing topics from inclusive hiring practices to overcoming entrepreneurial anxiety and financial wellness programs. Her published dissertation- focusing on the need for financial literacy in higher education- has been downloaded more than 225 times in 31 countries (as of November 2025).

Formerly a Vice President at Bank of America and a Director of Corporate Training in higher education, she now serves as a Real Estate Broker and CEO of The Dynasty Group and Senior Consultant for 5-Star Empowerment, where she blends her financial expertise with a passion for personal development. She is a past recipient of the San Antonio Top 100 Women Who's Who, and her influence has shaped legislation, academic policy, and financial curriculum statewide.

Whether speaking in the boardroom, classroom, or sanctuary, Dr. Weathersby is known for her straightforward, faith-infused, and actionable approach to transforming lives and legacies.

For Speaking Inquiries Contact:
Melissa@MelissaWeathersby.com
www.MelissaWeathersby.com

San Antonio, TX | 210.727.4127

Connect with me on Social Media!

Facebook: @TheDrMel
IG: @DrMelissaWeathersby
LinkedIn: in/melissaweathersby/

INTRODUCTION

This devotional was birthed in prayer. It is a 100-day journey designed to strengthen your faith, restore your focus, and awaken your prophetic vision.

Each day invites you to reflect, declare, and align with God's promises in both your spiritual and natural life. Take time to meditate on the Scriptures, journal your thoughts, and invite the Holy Spirit to breathe fresh revelation into your reading.

Remember, the goal is not perfection; it's progress. You're being perfected in His presence. As you go through these pages, may your spirit be lifted, your faith expanded, and your divine assignment made clear. Fasten your seatbelt! It's time to take flight in faith.

Day 1: Purpose in Service

Quote: *"When you know your purpose, every act of service carries meaning."*

Scripture: "Whatever you do, work at it with all your heart, as working for the Lord, not for human masters." -Colossians 3:23

Reflection: Every flight has a destination, and so does every life. As flight attendants, your role carries a higher purpose than just tasks: it's about serving with excellence as unto the Lord. Purpose transforms routine into mission.

Personal Application:

Today, remind yourself that even the smallest act of service is an offering to God. Carry out each responsibility as if serving Him directly. Consider what aspect of your service you love most. Write about why it resonates with you personally and how it shapes your identity as a flight attendant.

_____

_____

_____

_____

_____

_____

_____

_____

_____

_____

Prayer: Lord, thank You for the privilege of serving others. Help me to see my role as a meaningful opportunity to bring joy and comfort to those I encounter. Give me clarity of purpose and joy in service. May my work reflect my devotion to You.

Day 2: The Power of Kindness

Quote: *"Kindness can transform a passenger's experience."*

Scripture: *"A kind word is like honey; sweet to the soul and healthy for the body."* -Proverbs 16:24

Reflection: Kindness is a vital ingredient in customer service, offering warmth and comfort to those in transit. Reflect on how your acts of kindness can create a more favorable atmosphere during flights.

Personal Application:

Plan to perform at least one intentional act of kindness on your next flight. Consider how this small gesture can have a ripple effect throughout the cabin.

_____

_____

_____

_____

_____

_____

_____

_____

_____

_____

Prayer: Father, help me to embody kindness in my interactions. May my words and actions uplift others, creating a positive atmosphere on every flight.

Day 3: Navigating Challenges with Grace

Quote: *"Turbulence may shake the plane, but grace steadies the heart."*

Scripture: "But he said to me, 'My grace is sufficient for you, for my power is made perfect in weakness.'" -2 Corinthians 12:9

Reflection: Flight attendants often face unexpected challenges, much like turbulence in the skies. Reflect on how grace can help you navigate these moments with composure and strength, maintaining a reassuring presence for passengers.

Personal Application:

Think of a recent challenge you encountered in your role. How can you apply grace in similar situations moving forward?

_____

_____

_____

_____

_____

_____

_____

_____

_____

_____

Prayer: Lord, grant me the strength to handle challenges with grace. Let Your calmness flow through me, providing comfort to those around me in turbulent times.

Day 4: The Gift of Attention

Quote: *"Being attentive to passengers creates a welcoming environment."*

Scripture: Let each of you look not only to his own interests, but also to the interests of others. -Philippians 2:4

Reflection: Attention to detail and to the needs of passengers fosters a sense of belonging and safety. Reflect on the importance of being attentive and how it enhances the travel experience for everyone on board.

Personal Application:

Make it a point to engage with passengers during your next flight. Look for opportunities to offer support or assistance to someone who may need it.

Above The Clouds: 100 Daily Devotions For Flight Attendants

Prayer: Heavenly Father, help me to be attentive to the needs of passengers. Help me stay attentive to both spoken and unspoken needs May I serve with an open heart, recognizing the importance of each individual journey.

Day 5: Strength in Teamwork

Quote: *"Together with your crew, you can achieve seamless service."*

Scripture: "Two are better than one because they have a more satisfying return for their labor; for if either of them falls, the one will lift up his companion. But woe to him who is alone when he falls and does not have another to lift him up." -Ecclesiastes 4:9-10

Reflection: Teamwork is essential in ensuring a successful flight. Reflect on the dynamics of working together with your crew and how collaboration fosters unity and excellence in service.

Personal Application:

Reach out to a crew member you haven't interacted with recently. Strengthen your professional bond by acknowledging their contributions and working together effectively.

Prayer: Lord, bless the teamwork amongst my crew. Help us to support one another, serving together with harmony and purpose as we care for our passengers.

Day 6: Building Community Trust

Quote: *"Trust is key to a positive flying experience."*

Scripture: "Trust [rely on and have confidence] in the Lord and do good; Dwell in the land and feed [securely] on His faithfulness. -Psalm 37:3

Reflection: Building trust with passengers enhances their travel experience and fosters a sense of security. Reflect on how your interactions can contribute to a climate of trust and reassurance on your flights.

Personal Application:

Consider ways you can actively build trust with passengers. Perhaps begin with a smile, ensuring each interaction is warm and welcoming. Aim to provide clarifications and attentive responses to passenger inquiries.

_____

_____

_____

_____

_____

_____

_____

_____

_____

_____

Prayer: Heavenly Father, help me to cultivate trust with every passenger on board. As I serve, may my demeanor and actions reassure them of their safety and comfort.

Day 7: Finding Joy in Service

Quote: *"Joy in serving spreads like a warm breeze through the cabin."*

Scripture: "The joy of the Lord is your strength." -Nehemiah 8:10

Reflection: Your joy in serving can significantly influence the atmosphere on a flight, uplifting both passengers and crew. Reflect on the moments that bring you joy in your role and how sharing that joy with others can enhance everyone's experience.

Personal Application:

Today, focus on finding joy in the small moments of service. What makes you smile as you perform your duties? Share that joy with your colleagues and passengers.

Prayer: Lord, fill my heart with joy. May my positive energy uplift those around me and create a delightful atmosphere throughout the flight.

Day 8: Resilience in Tough Situations

Quote: *"Resilience is key in handling in-flight challenges."*

Scripture: *"I can do all things through Christ who strengthens me." -Philippians 4:13*

Reflection: Challenges can arise unexpectedly in the air. Reflect on your resilience and strength during difficult moments, remembering that you have the capacity to handle adversity.

Personal Application:

Identify a recent challenge you faced while serving. Write down how you handled or overcame it and what lessons you can apply in the future.

_____

_____

_____

_____

_____

_____

_____

_____

_____

_____

Prayer: Father, thank You for giving me strength in tough moments. Help me to remember that I can rely on You for resilience in every challenge I encounter.

Day 9: The Value of Professionalism

Quote: *"Professionalism reflects our commitment to excellence."*

Scripture: "Whatever you do, work at it with all your heart." -Colossians 3:23

Reflection: Demonstrating professionalism in your service enhances the reputation of your airline and instills confidence in passengers. Reflect on the importance of maintaining high standards in your work.

Personal Application:

Today, choose one area where you can enhance your professionalism: in your appearance, communication, or approach to service. Note how it affects your interactions.

_____

_____

_____

_____

_____

_____

_____

_____

_____

_____

Prayer: Lord, guide me to uphold professionalism in all that I do. May my conduct reflect my commitment to excellence and inspire confidence in those I serve.

Day 10: Embracing Cultural Diversity

Quote: *"Embrace the diversity of passengers; it enriches your service."*

Scripture: *"For we are all one in Christ Jesus."* - Galatians 3:28

Reflection: Working with diverse passengers offers insights and enriches your service experience. Reflect on how embracing this diversity within your crew and the passengers can lead to greater understanding and acceptance.

Personal Application:

Strive to learn something new about a culture represented among your passengers. Engage someone in conversation about their background and experiences.

_____

_____

_____

_____

_____

_____

_____

_____

_____

_____

Prayer: Heavenly Father, help me embrace the diversity around me. May I honor each individual and learn to serve everyone with respect and appreciation for their uniqueness.

Day 11: The Comfort of Intentionality

Quote: *"Intentionality in interactions brings comfort and assurance."*

Scripture: "Let your conversation be always full of grace." -Colossians 4:6

Reflection: Being intentional in your interactions can provide comfort to anxious passengers. Reflect on how a thoughtful, genuine approach can alleviate stress and create a positive environment.

Personal Application:

During your next interaction, focus on being fully present. Listen attentively and respond with compassion to show your passengers they matter.

Prayer: Lord, guide me to be intentional in my service. Help me to provide comfort and assurance to each passenger through my words and actions.

Day 12: The Challenge of Conflict Resolution

Quote: *"Conflict resolution is an essential skill in service."*

Scripture: "If it is possible, as far as it depends on you, live at peace with everyone." -Romans 12:18

Reflection: Conflicts may arise during flights, requiring patience and skill to resolve. Reflect on your approach to conflict resolution and how maintaining peace is vital in the cabin environment.

Personal Application:

Identify a strategy you can use to approach conflict calmly. Consider how you can de-escalate tense situations to ensure a peaceful resolution.

_____

_____

_____

_____

_____

_____

_____

_____

_____

_____

Prayer: Father, grant me the wisdom and patience to handle conflicts gracefully. Help me to maintain an atmosphere of peace during challenging situations , and to guide others toward understanding and resolution.

Day 13: The Impact of Your Actions

Quote: *"Every action, no matter how small, contributes to the overall experience."*

Scripture: "So whether you eat or drink or whatever you do, do it all for the glory of God." - 1 Corinthians 10:31

Reflection: Recognizing that your actions influence the travel experience of passengers can lead to more mindful service. Reflect on how your daily choices, interactions, and demeanor collectively shape the atmosphere on a flight.

Personal Application:

Choose an opportunity today to perform a small act of service that boosts someone's experience, whether it's a kind word or thoughtful gesture. Pay attention to how it affects both them and you.

_____

_____

_____

_____

_____

_____

_____

_____

_____

_____

_____

Prayer: Lord, let my actions reflect Your love and light. Help me to serve with intention, knowing that every small action can create a significant impact on someone's journey.

Day 14: The Role of Team Spirit

Quote: *"Team spirit enhances our service delivery."*

Scripture: "As iron sharpens iron, so one person sharpens another." -Proverbs 27:17

Reflection: A strong sense of teamwork is essential in providing excellent service and ensuring passenger safety. Reflect on how you can cultivate team spirit among your colleagues and the importance of collaboration.

Personal Application:

Take a moment to acknowledge a teammate and express gratitude for their support. Consider planning a small team-building activity or simply sharing a meal together after a flight.

_____

_____

_____

_____

_____

_____

_____

_____

_____

_____

Prayer: Heavenly Father, help me to foster a spirit of teamwork with my colleagues. May we support and uplift one another, creating a cohesive and positive environment for all.

Day 15: The Seat of Empathy

Quote: *"Empathy transforms passenger experiences."*

Scripture: "Rejoice with those who rejoice; mourn with those who mourn." -Romans 12:15

Reflection: Empathy allows you to connect with passengers on a deeper level, showing that you understand their experiences and emotions. Reflect on how your ability to empathize can enhance service quality and passenger satisfaction.

Personal Application:

During interactions, practice active listening. Try to genuinely understand the emotions and needs of passengers, particularly those who may be anxious or upset.

Prayer: Lord, cultivate empathy in my heart. Help me to connect with each passenger genuinely, understanding their needs and experiences with compassion.

Day 16: Celebrating Small Victories

Quote: *"Every small victory counts."*

Scripture: "Do not despise these small beginnings, for the Lord rejoices to see the work begin." -Zechariah 4:10

Reflection: Acknowledging and celebrating small victories can boost morale and motivation. Reflect on recent successes in your role as a flight attendant and how they contribute to the overall mission.

Personal Application:

Make a list of recent accomplishments in your work, no matter how small. Share these with your team or keep them in a journal as reminders of your progress.

Prayer: Father, thank You for the victories I have experienced in my role. Help me to recognize the significance of each success, reinforcing my dedication to service.

Day 17: The Art of Adaptability

Quote: *"Flexibility is key in a dynamic environment."*

Scripture: "In their hearts, humans plan their course, but the Lord establishes their steps." - Proverbs 16:9

Reflection: Traveling often involves unexpected changes and challenges. Reflect on how being adaptable enhances your ability to meet passengers' needs and create positive experiences, even in uncertainty.

Personal Application:

Identify an area where you struggled with adaptability recently. Consider a strategy you can adopt to help you remain flexible and open-minded moving forward.

_____

_____

_____

_____

_____

_____

_____

_____

_____

_____

Prayer: Lord, help me to embrace adaptability in my role. Enable me to respond to changes with grace and confidence, ensuring that I meet the needs of my passengers effectively.

Day 18: The Gift of Graciousness

Quote: *"Graciousness fosters goodwill among passengers."*

Scripture: "Let your conversation be always full of grace." -Colossians 4:6

Reflection: Practicing graciousness can create a welcoming environment on the flight. Reflect on how a gracious attitude can alleviate tensions and enhance interactions with passengers.

Personal Application:

Make a point to express graciousness in your interactions today. Whether it's thanking passengers for their patience or acknowledging their preferences, notice how this impacts their journey.

Prayer: Heavenly Father may my words and actions reflect graciousness. Help me to create a warm atmosphere that brings comfort and joy to passengers during their travels.

Day 19: The Power of Forgiveness

Quote: *"Forgiveness can clear the path for positive interactions."*

Scripture: *"Forgive as the Lord forgave you."* - Colossians 3:13

Reflection: As a flight attendant, you may encounter challenging interactions that can lead to frustration or resentment. Reflect on how practicing forgiveness can not only relieve you of emotional burdens but also create a more pleasant environment for both you and your passengers.

Personal Application:

Identify any grudges you might be holding, whether against a passenger or a colleague. Make a conscious decision to forgive, allowing that burden to lift and opening up space for more positive interactions.

_____

_____

_____

_____

_____

_____

_____

_____

_____

_____

Prayer: Lord, help me to embody forgiveness in my heart. Grant me the strength to let go of past grievances, enabling a fresh start and uplifting atmosphere in my service.

Day 20: The Gift of a Friendly Smile

Quote: *"A smile is a universal sign of warmth and approachability."*

Scripture: *"A cheerful look brings joy to the heart; good news makes for good health."* - Proverbs 15:30

Reflection: A simple smile can have a profound impact on passengers, easing anxiety and creating a welcoming atmosphere. Reflect on the power of your smile and its ability to communicate reassurance and friendliness.

Personal Application:

Make a point to greet every passenger with a smile during your next flight. Observe how this small gesture influences their mood and creates a more positive environment in the cabin.

Prayer: Heavenly Father, remind me of the power of a simple smile. May I bring joy and reassurance to each passenger I encounter, reflecting Your love and grace.

Day 21: The Legacy of Service

Quote: *"Your service leaves a lasting impact on those you encounter."*

Scripture: "A good person leaves an inheritance for their children's children." -Proverbs 13:22

Reflection: Your dedication to serving others creates a legacy that extends beyond individual flights. Reflect on the long-term effects your kindness, patience, and professionalism can have on passengers and the broader community.

Personal Application:

Write down the qualities you want to embody in your service. Consider how these traits can leave a positive legacy for future generations of flight attendants and travelers.

_____

_____

_____

_____

_____

_____

_____

_____

_____

_____

_____

Prayer: Lord, help me to be mindful of the legacy I create through my service. May my actions today inspire and uplift, leaving a positive impact long after the flight has landed.

Day 22: Embracing Diversity

Quote: *"Diversity enriches our work environment and passenger experiences."*

Scripture: "For we are not all the same body but many parts; we all belong to one another." - Romans 12:5

Reflection: Embracing the diversity of passengers not only enriches service but also fosters understanding and acceptance. Reflect on how different cultures, backgrounds, and perspectives can enhance the travel experience for everyone involved.

Personal Application:

Take time to learn about the cultures of the passengers you may serve. Consider engaging someone on your next flight to learn about their background and experiences.

Prayer: Heavenly Father, help me appreciate the diversity within my cabin. May my interactions reflect respect and understanding, enhancing the experience for everyone onboard.

Day 23: The Importance of Communication

Quote: *"Clear communication is vital for effective service."*

Scripture: *"*Let your speech always be gracious, seasoned with salt.*"* -Colossians 4:6

Reflection: Effective communication is crucial in addressing the needs and concerns of passengers. Reflect on how the clarity of your words can foster understanding and enhance the overall travel experience.

Personal Application:

Focus on using clear and concise communication during your next flight. Practice active listening to ensure passengers feel heard and valued.

Prayer: Lord, guide my words and communication. Help me convey information with clarity and kindness, ensuring passengers feel attended to and respected.

Day 24: The Gift of Compassion

Quote: *"Compassion can turn a stressful trip into a memorable journey."*

Scripture: "Therefore, as God's chosen people, holy and dearly loved, clothe yourselves with compassion." -Colossians 3:12

Reflection: Compassion in your service helps passengers feel valued and cared for, especially during stressful travel times. Reflect on how you can embody compassion in your interactions and the difference it can make.

Personal Application:

Identify an opportunity to express compassion today, whether it's through listening, assisting a passenger with a need, or simply offering encouragement.

_____

_____

_____

_____

_____

_____

_____

_____

_____

_____

Prayer: Father, fill my heart with compassion. Guide me to connect with passengers genuinely, providing comfort and care whenever they need it.

Day 25: The Strength of Teamwork

Quote: *"Together, we achieve more."*

Scripture: "Two are better than one, because they have a good return for their labor." - Ecclesiastes 4:9

Reflection: Flight attendants rely on one another to deliver exceptional service and ensure safety onboard. Reflect on the strength found in teamwork and how it enhances your ability to provide outstanding service.

Personal Application:

Identify a colleague you can support today. Offer assistance, share feedback, or simply express your appreciation for their contributions to the team.

_____

_____

_____

_____

_____

_____

_____

_____

_____

_____

Prayer: Lord, bless the teamwork among our crew. May we support one another and create a harmonious environment that benefits both our passengers and ourselves.

Day 26: The Impact of a Positive Attitude

Quote: *"A positive attitude is contagious."*

Scripture: "The cheerful heart has a continual feast." -Proverbs 15:15

Reflection: Your attitude can influence the atmosphere in the cabin, impacting both crew morale and passenger experience. Reflect on how maintaining a positive outlook can uplift those around you.

Personal Application:

Before your next flight, take a moment to set a positive intention for the day. Notice how a positive attitude affects your interactions with passengers and colleagues.

_____

_____

_____

_____

_____

_____

_____

_____

_____

_____

Prayer: Heavenly Father, help me to carry a positive attitude into my service. May my joy uplift others and create a pleasant atmosphere for everyone on board.

Day 27: The Art of Patience

Quote: *"Patience is essential in the service industry."*

Scripture: "Be completely humble and gentle; be patient, bearing with one another in love." - Ephesians 4:2

Reflection: The nature of your work often demands patience, whether it's with a passenger needing extra assistance or during unforeseen flight delays. Reflect on the value of patience and how it can improve your service.

Personal Application:

During a busy or stressful time today, practice patience. Take a deep breath and remind yourself that your calmness can positively affect both yourself and those around you.

Prayer: Lord, grant me patience in my service, especially during challenging moments. Help me to respond with grace and understanding when needed most.

Day 28: The Importance of Safety

Quote: *"Safety is our top priority."*

Scripture: "The Lord will keep you safe from all harm- he will watch over your life." -Psalm 121:7

Reflection: Ensuring the safety of passengers is a fundamental part of your responsibilities. Reflect on the protocols and practices that contribute to a secure and safe travel environment.

Personal Application:

Review safety protocols and consider how you can reinforce them in your daily routines. Think of ways to encourage the crew and passengers to prioritize their safety during the flight.

_____

_____

_____

_____

_____

_____

_____

_____

_____

_____

Prayer: Heavenly Father, guide my actions to prioritize safety at all times. May my diligence ensure a secure environment for every passenger I serve.

Day 29: Empowering Other Crew Members

Quote: *"Empower your crew to share ideas and feedback."*

Scripture: "Iron sharpens iron, and one man sharpens another." -Proverbs 27:17

Reflection: Encouraging your colleagues to share their insights leads to better teamwork and service. Reflect on how empowerment fosters a culture of collaboration and innovation.

Personal Application:

Create an opportunity for your team to share feedback or ideas, perhaps during a pre-flight meeting. Acknowledge their contributions to strengthen team dynamics.

_____

_____

_____

_____

_____

_____

_____

_____

_____

Prayer: Lord, help me to encourage and empower those I work with. May our collaboration foster creativity and improve the service we provide to our passengers.

Day 30: Celebrating Each Flight

Quote: *"Every flight is a new adventure."*

Scripture: "This is the day the Lord has made; let us rejoice and be glad in it." -Psalm 118:24

Reflection: Each flight presents an opportunity for new experiences, relationships, and memories. Reflect on how approaching each journey with excitement can enhance your perspective and service.

Personal Application:

Before each flight, take a moment to celebrate the unique opportunity ahead. Consider how you can make this journey special for yourself and your passengers.

_____

_____

_____

_____

_____

_____

_____

_____

_____

_____

Prayer: Heavenly Father, thank You for the opportunity to serve on each flight. Help me to embrace every journey with joy and to create memorable experiences for all those on board.

Day 31: The Legacy of Your Service

Quote: *"Your positive influence can leave a lasting legacy."*

Scripture: "A good person leaves an inheritance for their children's children." -Proverbs 13:22

Reflection: Reflect on the impact your service has on passengers and how your actions can contribute to a lasting legacy within the community and the industry. Each flight is an opportunity to create memories and foster goodwill, shaping how others perceive the role of flight attendants.

Personal Application:

Think about the legacy you want to leave behind. Write down a few ways your service can inspire future generations of flight attendants and travelers alike.

_____

_____

_____

_____

_____

_____

_____

_____

_____

_____

Prayer: Lord, may my service today contribute to a legacy of kindness, safety, and excellence. Help me to be a positive influence in the lives of those I encounter, leaving them with uplifting memories of their journey.

Day 32: The Importance of Reflection

Quote: *"Self-reflection fosters personal growth."*

Scripture: "Examine yourselves to see whether you are in the faith; test yourselves." -2 Corinthians 13:5

Reflection: Taking time for self-reflection allows you to evaluate your experiences and growth as a flight attendant. Reflect on how these moments of introspection can help you improve your service and personal well-being.

Personal Application:

Set aside time after each trip to jot down reflections on what went well and what you can improve. Use this journal for ongoing personal development.

_____

_____

_____

_____

_____

_____

_____

_____

_____

_____

Prayer: Heavenly Father, guide my self-reflection practice. Help me to learn from my experiences and become a more effective and compassionate flight attendant.

Day 33: The Gift of Patience

Quote: *"Patience transforms challenges into opportunities."*

Scripture: "Rejoice in hope, be patient in tribulation, be constant in prayer." -Romans 12:12

Reflection: Travel can be unpredictable, and patience is essential in your role, particularly during delays or passenger frustrations. Reflect on how maintaining a patient demeanor can enhance both your experience and that of your passengers.

Personal Application:

When faced with a challenging situation, consciously take a deep breath and practice patience. Write about how this impacts your response and the overall atmosphere onboard.

_____

_____

_____

_____

_____

_____

_____

_____

_____

_____

_____

Prayer: Lord, grant me the patience to navigate the ups and downs of my job. Help me to remain calm and composed, providing reassurance to passengers during stressful moments.

Day 34: The Power of a Good Attitude

Quote: *"A positive attitude can shift the atmosphere."*

Scripture: "A joyful heart is good medicine, but a crushed spirit dries up the bones." -Proverbs 17:22

Reflection: Your attitude significantly influences the mood of passengers and crew alike. Reflect on how maintaining a positive outlook can uplift those around you, creating a more enjoyable travel experience.

Personal Application:

Identify a negative thought you've had recently. Consciously reframe it into a positive one. Notice how this shift affects your actions and interactions.

Prayer: Heavenly Father, help me to cultivate a positive attitude in my service. May my joy be infectious, uplifting those around me and creating a delightful atmosphere onboard.

Day 35: Kindness as a Transformative Tool

Quote: *"Kindness has the power to change a stressful experience into a pleasant one."*

Scripture: *"Let all that you do be done in love."* - 1 Corinthians 16:14

Reflection: Kindness is a transformative force that can ease anxieties and foster connection. Reflect on how your acts of kindness can significantly alter the passenger experience and strengthen your interactions.

Personal Application:

Plan a specific act of kindness to perform during your next flight. It could be as simple as helping a passenger with their luggage or offering an extra snack.

Prayer: Lord, help me to be a source of kindness in my interactions. Allow my love for others to shine through, transforming flights into joyous experiences for everyone involved.

Day 36: Building Bonds with Passengers

Quote: *"Creating connections enriches the travel experience."*

Scripture: "As each has received a gift, use it to serve one another." -1 Peter 4:10

Reflection: Each passenger has a unique story. Building connections enhances their journey and fosters a sense of community onboard. Reflect on how you can create meaningful interactions through your service.

Personal Application:

During your next flight, try to engage a passenger in conversation. Ask about their journey or interests and share a bit of yourself in return, fostering a genuine connection.

Prayer: Heavenly Father, help me to create authentic connections with passengers. May my efforts make their journeys more enjoyable and memorable.

Day 37: Collaborating with Your Team

Quote: *"Teamwork enhances flight safety and service quality."*

Scripture: "For we are all one body, many parts yet one together." -1 Corinthians 12:12

Reflection: Collaboration with your fellow crew members is essential for safety and service excellence. Reflect on how effective teamwork enhances your ability to meet passenger needs and how you can actively contribute to a collaborative environment.

Personal Application:

This week, focus on ways to support your teammates actively. Whether it's offering assistance, sharing responsibilities, or providing positive feedback, recognize that teamwork strengthens the entire crew.

Prayer: Lord, bless the teamwork among my crew. Help us to work together harmoniously, supporting each other in our shared mission to provide outstanding service.

Day 38: Acknowledging Passenger Experiences

Quote: *"Every passenger brings a unique perspective."*

Scripture: "Everyone should be quick to listen, slow to speak and slow to become angry." - James 1:19

Reflection: Understanding and acknowledging each passenger's unique experiences enriches the way you serve. Reflect on how active listening can promote empathy and connection during flights.

Personal Application:

Practice active listening on your next flight. Focus on understanding passengers' needs and feelings, allowing space for them to share their stories.

Prayer: Heavenly Father, grant me the ability to listen actively and empathetically. Help me to understand the perspectives of passengers, fostering connections that enrich their travel experience.

Day 39: The Role of Humility

Quote: *"Humility fosters grace in service."*

Scripture: "Humble yourselves before the Lord, and he will lift you up." -James 4:10

Reflection: Serving with humility allows you to prioritize the needs of your passengers above your own. Reflect on how humility enhances your interactions and promotes a culture of respect on board.

Personal Application:

Look for opportunities this week to practice humility in your service. Whether taking the time to assist a colleague or being patient with a demanding passenger, recognize the strength in humility.

Prayer: Lord, teach me the power of humility in my service. Help me to place the needs of others above my own, reflecting Your love and grace to everyone around me.

Day 40: The Importance of Empathy

Quote: *"Empathy transforms service into a personal connection."*

Scripture: "Carry each other's burdens, and in this way you will fulfill the law of Christ." - Galatians 6:2

Reflection: Empathy allows you to understand the emotional journeys of passengers, creating a deeper connection. Reflect on how your empathetic responses can significantly impact someone's travel experience.

Personal Application:

During your next flight, make a conscious effort to empathize with a passenger showing signs of stress or discomfort. Offer them comfort and reassurance where you can.

Prayer: Heavenly Father, instill in me a spirit of empathy. Help me to connect with passengers on a deeper level, showing them love and understanding during their journey.

Day 41: Celebrating Team Achievements

Quote: *"Recognition boosts morale and creates a positive environment."*

Scripture: "Be devoted to one another in love. Honor one another above yourselves." -Romans 12:10

Reflection: Recognizing your colleagues' efforts reinforces a supportive and positive workplace culture. Reflect on how celebrating achievements can enhance team spirit and motivation.

Personal Application:

Take a moment this week to acknowledge a colleague's hard work, whether through a verbal compliment or a small gesture. Recognize how this fosters goodwill within the team.

_____

_____

_____

_____

_____

_____

_____

_____

_____

_____

Prayer: Lord, help me to celebrate the achievements of my teammates. May my words of encouragement uplift them and strengthen our bond as a crew.

Day 42: The Impact of Professionalism

Quote: *"Professionalism reflects our commitment to passengers."*

Scripture: "Whatever you do, do it all for the glory of God." -1 Corinthians 10:31

Reflection: Maintaining professionalism is paramount in creating a safe and respectful environment. Reflect on how professionalism enhances trust between you and your passengers.

Personal Application:

Assess an area of your service where you can improve professionalism: whether in appearance, communication, or behavior. Set specific goals for improvement.

_____

_____

_____

_____

_____

_____

_____

_____

_____

_____

Prayer: Father, help me to uphold professionalism in every aspect of my service. May my commitment to excellence reflect Your glory and inspire confidence in those I serve.

Day 43: The Value of Safety

Quote: *"Safety is our primary responsibility."*

Scripture: "The Lord will keep you safe from all harm; he will watch over your life." –Psalm 121:7

Reflection: As a flight attendant, ensuring passenger safety is your foremost duty. Reflect on how your dedication to safety reassures passengers and enhances their overall experience.

Personal Application:

Review safety protocols and take stock of your responsibilities. Consider one area where you can improve to ensure that safety remains a top priority on every flight.

_____

_____

_____

_____

_____

_____

_____

_____

_____

_____

_____

Prayer: Heavenly Father, guide my actions as I prioritize safety in my role. May my diligence instill confidence in those I serve and help create a secure atmosphere for every journey.

Day 44: The Importance of Reflection

Quote: "Self-reflection allows for growth and understanding."

Scripture: "Examine yourselves to see whether you are in the faith; test yourselves." -2 Corinthians 13:5

Reflection: Regular self-reflection is essential in any profession, especially in a service-oriented field like flight attendants. Reflect on how reflecting on your actions and experiences can enhance your effectiveness and personal growth.

Personal Application:

After each flight, take a few moments to jot down your thoughts on what went well and what could be improved. Use this journal as a tool for ongoing development.

_____

_____

_____

_____

_____

_____

_____

_____

_____

_____

Prayer: Lord, guide my self-reflection. Help me to learn from my experiences and grow in my capacity to serve others effectively.

Day 45: The Impact of Positive Engagement

Quote: *"Positive engagement creates memorable journeys."*

Scripture: "Let your lips be a fountain of life." - Proverbs 10:11

Reflection: Engaging positively with passengers enhances their experience and creates lasting memories. Reflect on how your approachability and enthusiasm can significantly influence the atmosphere on board.

Personal Application:

Focus on how you can make each passenger feel valued during the flight. Consider what small, positive interactions you can have that might enhance their experience.

_____

_____

_____

_____

_____

_____

_____

_____

_____

_____

Above The Clouds: 100 Daily Devotions For Flight Attendants

Prayer: Heavenly Father, let me be a source of positivity in every interaction. May my enthusiasm and warm engagement uplift passengers and create memorable journeys.

Day 46: The Art of Patience

Quote: *"Patience is essential in delivering excellent service."*

Scripture: "Be completely humble and gentle; be patient, bearing with one another in love." - Ephesians 4:2

Reflection: Flight attendants require patience, whether dealing with challenging passengers or unforeseen delays. Reflect on how patience can not only improve your experience but also enhance the overall atmosphere for everyone on board.

Personal Application:

When faced with a demanding situation on your next flight, consciously practice patience. Notice how this change affects your demeanor and influence on passengers.

Prayer: Lord, grant me the patience I need while I serve. Help me to respond with calmness and grace, creating a positive experience for my passengers.

Day 47: Practicing Empathy

Quote: *"Empathy transforms interactions and fosters connection."*

Scripture: "Rejoice with those who rejoice; mourn with those who mourn." -Romans 12:15

Reflection: Connecting with passengers on an emotional level enhances your ability to provide comfort and support during flights. Reflect on how practicing empathy can transform your interactions and deepen relationships.

Personal Application:

During your next interaction, focus on actively listening and genuinely understanding the passenger's perspective. Notice how this fosters a deeper connection.

Prayer: Heavenly Father, fill me with empathy for those I serve. Help me to connect with each passenger on a deeper level, making their experience more meaningful and comforting.

Day 48: The Power of a Grateful Heart

Quote: *"Gratitude changes your perspective."*

Scripture: "Give thanks in all circumstances; for this is the will of God in Christ Jesus for you." – 1 Thessalonians 5:18

Reflection: Practicing gratitude helps you maintain a positive outlook, even in challenging situations. Reflect on the benefits of acknowledging the small blessings in your daily work.

Personal Application:

Start a gratitude journal and list three things you're thankful for at work each day. Notice how this practice affects your mood and the way you approach your service.

Prayer: Lord, thank You for the opportunity to serve. Help me to develop a grateful heart and recognize the blessings in my role as a flight attendant.

Day 49: Nurturing Professional Relationships

Quote: *"Building strong relationships enhances teamwork."*

Scripture: "As iron sharpens iron, so one person sharpens another." -Proverbs 27:17

Reflection: Strong relationships among crew members contribute to effective teamwork and a supportive work environment. Reflect on the relationships you've built and how they contribute to job satisfaction and success.

Personal Application:

Take time today to compliment a colleague or express appreciation for their support. Notice how strengthening these connections benefits morale and cooperation on your team.

Prayer: Heavenly Father, help me to foster strong relationships with my fellow crew members. May our teamwork enrich our service and create a positive environment for everyone.

Day 50: The Role of Adaptability

Quote: *"Adaptability is essential in the flight industry."*

Scripture: *"In their hearts, humans plan their course, but the Lord establishes their steps."* - Proverbs 16:9

Reflection: The unpredictability of the aviation industry requires you to be adaptable in multiple scenarios. Reflect on how your ability to pivot and embrace change contributes to effective service in a rapidly shifting environment.

Personal Application:

Identify a recent situation where you had to adapt quickly. How did you respond, and what did you learn from it? Write down how you can apply those lessons to future situations.

_____

_____

_____

_____

_____

_____

_____

_____

_____

_____

Prayer: Lord, help me to embrace adaptability in my role. Guide me to respond positively to changes and challenges, ensuring that I can provide the best service possible in any situation.

Day 51: The Joy of Service

Quote: *"Finding joy in service enhances the travel experience for everyone."*

Scripture: "The joy of the Lord is your strength." -Nehemiah 8:10

Reflection: Serving others can bring immense joy, both to you and to those you are serving. Consider how your joyful attitude can influence the atmosphere on board, transforming an ordinary flight into an extraordinary experience.

Personal Application:

Create a personal mantra or affirmation about the joy of your work. Repeat it to yourself when you feel challenged or stressed during flights.

Prayer: Heavenly Father, fill my heart with joy as I serve. Help me to share that joy with passengers and colleagues, creating an environment of positivity on every journey.

Day 52: Coping with Stress

Quote: *"Finding ways to cope with stress enhances your performance."*

Scripture: *"Cast all your anxiety on him because he cares for you."* -1 Peter 5:7

Reflection: The aviation industry can be high-pressure and stressful. Reflect on the importance of managing stress effectively for your well-being and for the quality of service you provide.

Personal Application:

Identify a stress-relief technique that works for you, such as deep breathing, meditation, or physical activity. Commit to incorporating this into your routine, especially during busy flight days.

_____

_____

_____

_____

_____

_____

_____

_____

_____

_____

Prayer: Lord, help me to manage my stress and anxiety effectively. Give me the wisdom to seek peace in the midst of challenges and to find strength in You during turbulent times.

Day 53: The Art of Hospitality

Quote: *"Hospitality is at the heart of exceptional service."*

Scripture: "Share with the Lord's people who are in need. Practice hospitality." -Romans 12:13

Reflection: Your role as a flight attendant inherently involves hospitality. A welcoming attitude can significantly enhance a passenger's experience. Reflect on how embodying hospitality creates a reassuring and warm atmosphere.

Personal Application:

Plan a few ways to go above and beyond in your service, whether through small gestures or attentive interactions, to cultivate a hospitable environment on your next flight.

Prayer: Heavenly Father, thank You for the opportunity to show hospitality in my service. Help me to provide a welcoming and warm experience for every passenger on board.

Day 54: The Importance of Preparation

Quote: *"Preparation is key to a successful flight."*

Scripture: "A wise man thinks ahead; a fool doesn't and even brags about it!" -Proverbs 13:16 (TLB)

Reflection: Adequate preparation is crucial for ensuring everything runs smoothly in your role. Reflect on how being well-prepared can minimize stress and enhance your confidence on flights.

Personal Application:

Before your next flight, take extra time to prepare. This could include reviewing safety protocols, checking supplies, or mentally rehearsing customer interactions.

_____

_____

_____

_____

_____

_____

_____

_____

_____

_____

Prayer: Lord, help me to prepare diligently for my work. May my preparation lead to confidence and effective service during every flight.

Day 55: The Value of Feedback

Quote: *"Feedback fosters growth and improvement."*

Scripture: "Listen to advice and accept instruction, that you may gain wisdom in the future." -Proverbs 19:20

Reflection: Feedback is vital for personal and professional growth. Reflect on how accepting constructive criticism and seeking feedback from your peers can enhance your performance and relationships.

Personal Application:

After your next flight, ask a trusted colleague for feedback on your service. Reflect on their insights and how you can incorporate this feedback into your future work.

_____

_____

_____

_____

_____

_____

_____

_____

_____

_____

Prayer: Heavenly Father, guide me to be open to feedback and constructive criticism. Help me to use this as a tool for my growth, becoming a better flight attendant.

Day 56: The Impact of a Caring Touch

Quote: "A caring touch can create lasting connections."

Scripture: "And whoever welcomes one such child in my name welcomes me." -Matthew 18:5

Reflection: Genuine care in your interactions can create lasting connections with passengers. Reflect on how small gestures of kindness and care such as a reassuring pat on the shoulder or a comforting word can positively impact someone's travel experience.

Personal Application:

During your next flight, look for opportunities to offer not just verbal support, but also a caring touch or gesture that can reassure passengers who may need it.

Prayer: Lord, help me express genuine care in my service. May my actions bring comfort to those I serve, reminding them that they are valued and not alone on their journey.

Day 57: Finding Purpose in Every Flight

Quote: *"Each flight is an opportunity to serve with purpose."*

Scripture: "And whatever you do, whether in word or deed, do it all in the name of the Lord Jesus, giving thanks to God the Father through him." -Colossians 3:17

Reflection: Embracing the purpose behind each flight can enhance your sense of fulfillment in your role. Reflect on how your service extends beyond mechanical tasks, impacting lives, comforting souls, and making travel easier for others.

Personal Application:

Take a moment before each flight to remind yourself of the significance of your work. Consider writing down three reasons you are grateful for the opportunity to serve.

_____

_____

_____

_____

_____

_____

_____

_____

_____

_____

Prayer: Heavenly Father, help me to embrace the purpose of my service. May I approach each flight with gratitude and a focus on how I can make a positive impact on the lives of others.

Day 58: The Gift of Connections in the Air

Quote: *"Connecting with passengers enriches their journey."*

Scripture: "Encourage one another and build each other up." -1 Thessalonians 5:11

Reflection: Building connections with passengers transforms a simple flight into a memorable experience. Reflect on how fostering relationships not only uplifts your spirits but also brings joy to those traveling with you.

Personal Application:

Make it a goal to initiate a conversation with at least one passenger during your next flight. Ask about their travels or interests, and share something about yourself that creates a connection.

Prayer: Lord, help me to connect meaningfully with passengers. May my interactions foster warmth, encouragement, and a sense of community among those flying with me.

Day 59: The Journey of Professionalism

Quote: *"Professionalism is the foundation of excellent service."*

Scripture: "Whatever you do, do it all for the glory of God." -1 Corinthians 10:31

Reflection: Demonstrating professionalism enhances the reputation of your airline and instills confidence in passengers. Reflect on how your commitment to professionalism influences your interactions and the impression you leave.

Personal Application:

Identify one area where you can elevate your professionalism on the job, whether through improved communication, enhancing your appearance, or demonstrating knowledge about flight safety.

_____

_____

_____

_____

_____

_____

_____

_____

_____

_____

Prayer: Heavenly Father, guide my pursuit of professionalism in my role. May my dedication to quality service reflect Your glory and inspire trust in all whom I serve.

Day 60: Resilience Under Pressure

Quote: *"Resilience allows you to thrive in a challenging environment."*

Scripture: *"I can do all things through Christ who strengthens me."* -Philippians 4:13

Reflection: The nature of your work often brings high-pressure situations. Reflect on how resilience helps you manage stress while maintaining a positive attitude, which contributes to an enjoyable flight experience.

Personal Application:

When facing a stressful day or situation at work, remind yourself of your resilience. Write down a few affirmations that encourage you to remain strong and focused during challenging moments.

_____

_____

_____

_____

_____

_____

_____

_____

_____

_____

Prayer: Lord, grant me resilience in the face of challenges. Help me to remain strong and composed, providing exceptional service that uplifts others even in tough circumstances.

Day 61: The Importance of Adaptability

Quote: *"Being adaptable is key in a dynamic environment."*

Scripture: "A man's mind plans his way [as he journeys through life], But the Lord directs his steps *and* establishes them." – Proverbs 16:9

Reflection: Adaptability is essential in the fast-paced world of air travel, where changes can occur suddenly. Reflect on how being flexible in your approach enhances your ability to respond effectively to various situations.

Personal Application:

Identify a recent instance where you had to adapt quickly. Reflect on the experience and what you learned about staying calm in unexpected circumstances.

_____

_____

_____

_____

_____

_____

_____

_____

_____

Prayer: Heavenly Father, help me embrace adaptability in my work. Equip me with the strength to respond gracefully to changes and challenges that arise during flights.

Day 62: The Gift of Perspective

Quote: *"Seeing things from a passenger's perspective enhances service."*

Scripture: "Do to others as you would have them do to you." -Luke 6:31

Reflection: Understanding the passenger experience can transform service delivery. Reflect on how seeing things from the perspective of travelers helps you provide empathy and support, ultimately improving their journey.

Personal Application:

On your next flight, identify a passenger who appears anxious or distressed. Make a conscious effort to place yourself in their shoes and respond to their needs accordingly.

_____

_____

_____

_____

_____

_____

_____

_____

_____

_____

Prayer: Lord, grant me the insight to understand the experiences of my passengers. May my actions reflect a genuine desire to care for them, making their journeys more pleasant and comforting.

Day 63: The Gift of Empathy

Quote: *"Empathy allows us to see the journey through another's eyes."*

Scripture: "Let each of you look not only to his own interests, but also to the interests of others." -Philippians 2:4

Reflection: Empathy transforms ordinary service into extraordinary care. By learning to see through the eyes of others, we recognize needs we might otherwise overlook. For flight attendants, this perspective builds trust and comfort in the cabin. When we step outside our own point of view, we not only meet practical needs but also minister to the hearts of those we serve.

Personal Application:

Today, take notice of the unspoken cues around you: a hesitant glance, a tired expression, or a passenger who seems uneasy. Choose one moment to respond with compassion, showing that you are not only present but also attentive to their journey.

Prayer: Lord, open my eyes to the needs of those around me. Teach me to look beyond myself and to value others with the love and empathy You show to me. May my service reflect Your heart.

Day 64: The Importance of Communication

Quote: *"Together as a crew, your efforts multiply."*

Scripture: "Let your conversation be always full of grace, seasoned with salt." -Colossians 4:6

Reflection: Effective communication is vital in ensuring safety and enhancing passenger experience. Reflect on how clarity and kindness in communication contribute to building trust with passengers.

Personal Application:

During your service, practice active listening. Focus on ensuring your instructions are clear, polite, and respectful, and gauge passengers' understanding through questions.

_____

_____

_____

_____

_____

_____

_____

_____

_____

_____

Prayer: Lord, guide my words and tone as I communicate. Help me to convey messages clearly and graciously, promoting understanding and comfort among my passengers.

Day 65: Nurturing Your Purpose

Quote: *"Purpose turns routine tasks into sacred opportunities to shine your light."*

Scripture: "You are the light of the world. A town built on a hill cannot be hidden." -Matthew 5:14

Reflection: Recognizing the purpose behind your work brings deeper fulfillment. Reflect on how your role enables you to make a difference in people's lives, fostering a sense of purpose in your daily duties.

Personal Application:

Journal about the impact you hope to have on passengers' experiences. Set specific intentions for your service on your next flight that align with this purpose.

_____

_____

_____

_____

_____

_____

_____

_____

_____

_____

Prayer: Heavenly Father, help me to discover and embrace the purpose behind my service. May each flight reflect Your light and contribute positively to the lives of everyone on board.

Day 66: Learning from Experience

Quote: *"Finding purpose in service leads to fulfillment."*

Scripture: "And we know that in all things God works for the good of those who love him." - Romans 8:28

Reflection: Each flight can teach valuable lessons about service, culture, and human connection. Reflect on how embracing experiences- both positive and negative- can foster your growth as a flight attendant.

Personal Application:

After your next flight, take a moment to reflect on the day's events. Identify one lesson you learned and consider how you can apply it moving forward.

_____

_____

_____

_____

_____

_____

_____

_____

_____

_____

Prayer: Lord, guide me to learn from my experiences and grow through them. Help me to embrace every opportunity to develop as a flight attendant and as a person.

Day 67: The Impact of Your Actions

Quote: *"Every flight offers lessons for growth."*

Scripture: "Do not be deceived: God cannot be mocked. A man reaps what he sows." - Galatians 6:7

Reflection: Every action you take during service has a direct impact on the passengers and your crew. Reflect on the concept of accountability and how your choices can foster positive or negative experiences.

Personal Application:

Reflect on a recent decision in your service that affected others. Consider how you might adjust your actions to create a more beneficial environment next time.

_____

_____

_____

_____

_____

_____

_____

_____

_____

_____

Prayer: Father, help me to be mindful of my actions and their consequences. Guide me to choose wisely and serve in a way that uplifts and benefits those around me.

Day 68: The Strength of a Supportive Network

Quote: *"Your actions today shape the experiences of tomorrow."*

Scripture: "Two are better than one, because they have a good return for their labor - Ecclesiastes 4:9

Reflection: Strong relationships among crew members contribute to effective teamwork and a supportive work environment. Reflect on how enhancing these relationships can lead to improved service quality and job satisfaction.

Personal Application:

Make time to connect with a crew member you haven't engaged with recently. Share experiences and discuss how you can support each other in your roles.

Prayer: Heavenly Father, thank You for the support of my colleagues. Help us to strengthen each other through teamwork, enhancing our service to passengers and creating a positive workplace.

Day 69: The Impact of Teamwork

Quote: *"A supportive crew enhances the quality of service."*

Scripture: "For where two or three gather in my name, there am I with them." -Matthew 18:20

Reflection: Collaborative teamwork is vital for ensuring both safety and outstanding service. Reflect on how teamwork can elevate the quality of service provided and the atmosphere on board.

Personal Application:

During your next flight, look for opportunities to collaborate with your colleagues on tasks, enhancing communication and teamwork. Note how this strengthens your ability to serve passengers effectively.

Prayer: Lord, bless our teamwork in the cabin. Help us work together harmoniously, supporting one another and creating a positive experience for everyone on board.

Day 70: Nurturing a Culture of Support

Quote: *"Teamwork amplifies our effectiveness."*

Scripture: "And let us consider how we may spur one another on toward love and good deeds." -Hebrews 10:24

Reflection: Establishing a supportive environment among crew members fosters a culture of encouragement and improves service quality. Reflect on how you can contribute to this culture through your interactions and support.

Personal Application:

Reach out to a colleague who might need encouragement. Share thoughtful words or help them with a task to strengthen your team's culture of support.

Prayer: Heavenly Father, help me contribute to a culture of support among my colleagues. May my encouragement uplift others, fostering a harmonious and joyful atmosphere on our flights.

Day 71: The Art of Graceful Service

Quote: *"A culture of support enhances morale and service quality."*

Scripture: "Let your conversation be always full of grace, seasoned with salt, so that you may know how to answer everyone." -Colossians 4:6

Reflection: Providing service with grace and poise can transform a passenger's experience on-board. Reflect on how embracing grace improves your ability to navigate challenges while maintaining professional demeanor.

Personal Application:

During your next flight, consciously practice grace in your interactions, especially with difficult passengers. Observe how this affects your confidence and their reactions.

Prayer: Lord, grant me the grace to serve with poise. Help me navigate challenges with gentleness and kindness, creating a soothing experience for those I serve.

Day 72: The Importance of Presence

Quote: "Be present, be grateful, and make the most of the moment."

Scripture: Whatever your hand finds to do, do it with all your might.-Ecclesiastes 9:10

Reflection: Being present means giving your best in each moment, whether it's greeting passengers, assisting a colleague, or simply offering a smile. Scripture reminds us that every task- big or small- is an opportunity to serve wholeheartedly. When we are attentive and diligent, we not only honor God but also create a positive experience for those around us.

Personal Application:

Today, commit to approaching each responsibility with full focus and energy. Avoid rushing through tasks or treating them as routine. Instead, embrace each duty as a chance to bring excellence and grace into your service.

_____

_____

_____

_____

_____

_____

_____

_____

_____

_____

Prayer: Lord, help me to give my best in every moment. May I serve with diligence and a joyful heart, honoring You in all that I do.

Day 73: The Role of Innovation

Quote: *"Creativity is God's gift to us; using it is our gift back to Him."*

Scripture: "I, wisdom, dwell with prudence, and find out knowledge of witty inventions." – Proverbs 8:12

Reflection: Embracing creativity and innovation in your service can enhance the overall experience for passengers. Reflect on how thinking outside the box and introducing new ideas can create memorable flights.

Personal Application:

Brainstorm one innovative idea that could improve the passenger experience and discuss it with your team. Take steps to implement it during an upcoming flight.

Prayer: Lord, inspire my creativity as I serve. Help me embrace innovative solutions that lead to enriching experiences for passengers and my crew.

Day 74: Practicing Self-Care

Quote: "Self-care isn't selfish. It's sacred. Resting renews your ability to serve with grace."

Scripture: "Come to me, all you who are weary and burdened, and I will give you rest." - Matthew 11:28

Reflection: Taking care of your own well-being is crucial for providing exceptional service to others. Reflect on the importance of self-care and how it can recharge your spirit and energy during demanding shifts.

Personal Application:

Schedule a specific time for self-care this week, whether it's through exercise, meditation, reading, or engaging in a hobby you love. Acknowledge that caring for yourself allows you to serve better.

_____

_____

_____

_____

_____

_____

_____

_____

_____

_____

_____

Prayer: Heavenly Father, help me prioritize self-care in my life. May I find refreshment and energy so that I can serve others wholeheartedly and joyfully.

Day 75: The Rhythm of Rest

Quote: *"Rest is not a luxury; it is essential to serve well."*

Scripture: *"Then, because so many people were coming and going that they did not even have a chance to eat, he said to them, 'Come with me by yourselves to a quiet place and get some rest.'"* -Mark 6:31

Reflection: Even Jesus recognized the importance of rest for those serving alongside Him. Service that never pauses eventually leads to exhaustion and burnout. As a flight attendant, you carry significant responsibilities, but you can only give your best when you take time to renew your strength. Rest is not wasted time. It is God's design for replenishment so that you can continue to serve with joy, patience, and excellence.

Personal Application:

Today, schedule intentional moments of rest, even if brief. Use these times not only to recharge physically but also to reconnect spiritually. Allow yourself permission to pause, knowing that caring for your well-being honors God and equips you to serve others more effectively.

Prayer: Lord, teach me the value of rest. Help me to step away from constant demands and find renewal in Your presence. May my times of rest restore my strength so I can serve with clarity, compassion, and excellence.

Day 76: The Role of Gratitude

Quote: *"Gratitude reshapes how we serve."*

Scripture: "Give thanks in all circumstances; for this is the will of God in Christ Jesus for you." -1 Thessalonians 5:18

Reflection: Practicing gratitude can significantly influence your experience as a flight attendant. Reflect on the power of recognizing and appreciating the positives in your work, no matter the situation.

Personal Application:

Start a gratitude journal where you list three things you appreciate about your job each day. Notice how this practice impacts your mood and service quality.

_____

_____

_____

_____

_____

_____

_____

_____

_____

_____

Prayer: Father, thank You for the opportunity to serve. Help me cultivate a spirit of gratitude, recognizing the blessings in each flight and interaction.

Day 77: Learning from Feedback

Quote: *"Feedback is the breakfast of champions."* -Ken Blanchard

Scripture: "Listen to advice and accept instruction, that you may gain wisdom in the future." -Proverbs 19:20

Reflection: Seeking and incorporating feedback leads to continuous personal and professional growth. Reflect on how being open to constructive criticism encourages improvement in your role.

Personal Application:

After your next flight, ask for feedback from a trusted colleague. Reflect on their insights and how you can integrate their suggestions into your service.

Prayer: Lord, help me to embrace feedback as a tool for growth. Guide me to learn from others and continuously improve my service for the benefit of those I interact with.

Day 78: The Role of Humor

Quote: *"Laughter is medicine to the soul."*

Scripture: "A joyful heart is good medicine, but a crushed spirit dries up the bones." -Proverbs 17:22

Reflection: A sense of humor is a powerful tool for creating a positive atmosphere during flights. On long flights or in stressful moments, a genuine smile or shared laugh can shift the atmosphere, bringing comfort to passengers and strength to the crew. Laughter reminds us that joy is healing and that God designed our hearts to be renewed through it. Reflect on how light-heartedness can ease tension and foster connections both between crew members and with passengers.

Personal Application:

Look for opportunities to introduce humor into your interactions, especially during stressful times. Pay attention to how it influences the mood of both passengers and your crew. Share a smile, a kind word, or a gentle laugh that lifts the spirit of those around you.

_____

_____

_____

_____

_____

_____

_____

_____

_____

_____

Prayer: Lord, thank You for the gift of laughter. May I use it to bring healing, encouragement, and joy to those I serve. Fill my heart with cheerfulness that overflows into the lives of others. Amen.

Day 79: The Value of Empowerment

Quote: *"Empowering yourself and others fosters personal growth."*

Scripture: "As each has received a gift, use it to serve one another." -1 Peter 4:10

Reflection: Empowering yourself and your colleagues enhances teamwork and service quality. Reflect on how creating an environment that encourages growth leads to better outcomes for passengers.

Personal Application:

Identify a teammate who you can support by offering assistance or encouragement in their role. Consider sharing your insights or experiences that can help them in their service.

_____

_____

_____

_____

_____

_____

_____

_____

_____

_____

Prayer: Lord, help me empower those around me through support and encouragement. May we lift one another up, working together to ensure the best service for our passengers.

Day 80: The Influence of an Open Heart

Quote: *"An open heart leads to deeper connections."*

Scripture: *"Above all, love each other deeply, because love covers over a multitude of sins." –1 Peter 4:8*

Reflection: Approaching your role with an open heart helps you connect with passengers and crew alike. Reflect on how your willingness to form genuine relationships enhances the travel experience.

Personal Application:

Practice vulnerability in your interactions by sharing a little about yourself or showing concern for a passenger's feelings. This openness can foster meaningful connections.

Prayer: Father, help me to cultivate an open heart in my service. May my willingness to connect authentically with others create meaningful interactions and strengthen the bonds among passengers and colleagues alike.

Day 81: The Spirit of Giving

Quote: *"Service is a form of giving."*

Scripture: "It is more blessed to give than to receive." –Acts 20:35

Reflection: Each act of service reflects a spirit of generosity. Reflect on how your service, while fulfilling duties, also embodies the essence of giving to others: in care, attention, and support.

Personal Application:

Identify a way to go above and beyond the standard service expectations on your next flight. This could involve providing extra assistance or simply being extra attentive to a particular passenger.

Prayer: Lord, let my service be a genuine gift to those I encounter. Help me to embody the spirit of giving in my role, positively impacting everyone I serve.

Day 82: Navigating the Unknown

Quote: *"Navigating uncertainty requires courage and adaptability."*

Scripture: *"For I know the plans I have for you, declares the Lord, plans to prosper you and not to harm you, plans to give you hope and a future." -Jeremiah 29:11*

Reflection: A career in aviation is often filled with uncertainty. Reflect on how cultivating courage and adaptability can guide you through unexpected situations, ultimately contributing to effective management and passenger safety.

Personal Application:

When faced with an unpredictable situation, remind yourself of your ability to adapt. Write down strategies that can help you remain flexible and responsive in challenging environments.

_____

_____

_____

_____

_____

_____

_____

_____

_____

_____

Prayer: Heavenly Father, grant me the courage to face uncertainty with grace and adaptability. Help me to remain calm and focused, serving with poise during unexpected situations.

Day 83: Celebrating Team Strength

Quote: *"A united crew provides exceptional service."*

Scripture: *"How good and pleasant it is when God's people live together in unity!" -Psalm 133:1*

Reflection: The strength of your crew lies in unity and collaboration. Reflect on how fostering a sense of teamwork elevates service quality and creates a harmonious flying experience.

Personal Application:

Engage your crew in a team-building activity during downtime. Share experiences and develop stronger bonds that enhance teamwork during flights.

_____

_____

_____

_____

_____

_____

_____

_____

_____

_____

Prayer: Lord, bless our teamwork and unity as a crew. Help us to work cohesively in a spirit of service, ensuring the best experiences for our passengers.

Day 84: The Role of Continuous Improvement

Quote: *"Continuous improvement is key to exceptional service."*

Scripture: "Let all things be done decently and in order." -1 Corinthians 14:40

Reflection: Striving for continuous improvement enhances the travel experience for passengers and fosters a culture of excellence within the crew. Reflect on areas where you can implement improvements in your service delivery.

Personal Application:

Identify one area of your service where you believe improvements can be made. Develop a plan to optimize that aspect, whether it's communication or passenger assistance.

_____

_____

_____

_____

_____

_____

_____

_____

_____

_____

Prayer: Heavenly Father, guide my efforts for continuous improvement. Help me strive for excellence and to see the impact of my work on the experiences of my passengers.

Day 85: Finding Meaning in Challenges

Quote: *"Every challenge is an opportunity for growth."*

Scripture: "Consider it pure joy, my brothers and sisters, whenever you face trials of many kinds." -James 1:2

Reflection: Challenges in the aviation industry can serve as valuable lessons. Reflect on how embracing these challenges leads to personal and professional growth, enhancing your abilities as a flight attendant.

Personal Application:

Identify a recent challenge you faced while serving. Write down what you learned from that experience and how it has helped you to grow in your role.

_____

_____

_____

_____

_____

_____

_____

_____

_____

Prayer: Lord, help me to view challenges as opportunities for growth. May I learn from my experiences and develop resilience that enhances my service to others.

Day 86: The Value of Reflection

Quote: *"Reflection is essential for recognizing growth."*

Scripture: "Be still, and know that I am God." - Psalm 46:10

Reflection: Taking time to reflect on your journey as a flight attendant allows you to recognize personal growth and areas for improvement. Reflect on the importance of being still and allowing yourself to evaluate your experiences.

Personal Application:

Set aside time weekly for reflection. Use it to write in a journal about your experiences, feelings, and any lessons learned. This practice fosters personal growth.

Prayer: Heavenly Father, help me to create time for reflection in my life. May I learn from my experiences and recognize the growth You're guiding me through.

Day 87: The Importance of Self-Care

Quote: *"Self-care is not selfish; it is stewardship of the life God has given you."*

Scripture: "Come to me, all you who are weary and burdened, and I will give you rest." - Matthew 11:28

Reflection: Self-care is crucial for maintaining your energy and emotional well-being as a flight attendant. Reflect on your self-care practices and how they enable you to serve passengers effectively.

Personal Application:

Schedule time for self-care this week. Whether it's exercise, reading, or spending time with loved ones, prioritize activities that recharge your spirit.

_____

_____

_____

_____

_____

_____

_____

_____

_____

_____

Prayer: Lord, help me to prioritize self-care in my life. Remind me that taking care of myself allows me to serve others with more love and energy.

Day 88: The Value of Respectful Communication

Quote: *"True service begins with respect-for yourself and for others."*

Scripture: *"Let your conversation be always full of grace, seasoned with salt, so that you may know how to answer everyone."* -Colossians 4:6

Reflection: Words have power. They can build trust, ease tensions, or spark unnecessary conflict. Respectful communication goes beyond polite words; it reflects a heart that honors others. As a flight attendant, the tone you set through communication can shape the entire cabin atmosphere. When grace and respect guide your words, passengers and colleagues alike feel valued and safe.

Personal Application:

Today, practice speaking with intentional grace. Before responding, pause and consider whether your words reflect kindness, patience, and respect. Choose language that uplifts rather than diminishes.

Prayer: Lord, guide my words so that they honor You and respect others. Help me to communicate with clarity, compassion, and grace in every interaction.

Day 89: The Impact of Your Demeanor

Quote: *"Your attitude is a testimony others can read without words."*

Scripture: "Let your gentleness be evident to all. The Lord is near." –Philippians 4:5

Reflection: Your attitude and demeanor set the tone for the cabin environment. Reflect on how your positive energy can uplift passengers, especially when they may be feeling anxious.

Personal Application:

Be intentional about your demeanor on your next flight. Pay attention to how you carry yourself and the energy you bring to the cabin.

Prayer: Lord, fill me with positivity and cheer. Help me to be a source of comfort for passengers and colleagues alike, creating an atmosphere of joy and peace.

Day 90: The Importance of Observation

Quote: *"Observation opens our eyes to opportunities to serve."*

Scripture: "The prudent see danger and take refuge, but the simple keep going and pay the penalty." -Proverbs 22:3

Reflection: Your ability to observe the needs and emotions of passengers is crucial for effective service. Reflect on how keen observation can enhance your response to individual needs and create a more personalized experience.

Personal Application:

During your next flight, pay attention to the body language and cues from passengers. Note how this awareness allows you to better anticipate their needs.

Prayer: Father, grant me the insight to observe the needs of others. May I respond compassionately, ensuring that each passenger feels supported and cared for during their journey.

Day 91: Finding Balance Between Work and Life

Quote: *"Maintaining balance enhances overall well-being."*

Scripture: "There is a time for everything, and a season for every activity under the heavens." - Ecclesiastes 3:1

Reflection: Striving for balance between work and personal life is essential for your mental and emotional health. Reflect on how finding harmony in both areas can enhance your service.

Personal Application:

Assess how you can create more balance in your life. Make a plan to incorporate time for family, friends, and self-care alongside work commitments.

Prayer: Heavenly Father, help me find balance in my life. Guide me to prioritize both my service and personal well-being, ensuring I can thrive in all areas.

Day 92: The Influence of Your Heart

Quote: *"A heart of service transforms every interaction."*

Scripture: *"Above all else, guard your heart, for everything you do flows from it."* -Proverbs 4:23

Reflection: Your heart for service influences your actions and attitude. Reflect on the motivation behind your work and how a sincere heart can foster change in the experiences of those you serve.

Personal Application:

Take time today to reconnect with why you became a flight attendant. Write down your motivations and affirmations that reinforce your commitment to service.

_____

_____

_____

_____

_____

_____

_____

_____

_____

_____

Prayer: Lord, remind me of the importance of having a heart for service. May my love for others shine through in every interaction.

Day 93: The Importance of Gratitude

Quote: *"Gratitude can elevate your service to new heights."*

Scripture: "Give thanks in all circumstances; for this is the will of God in Christ Jesus for you." -1 Thessalonians 5:18

Reflection: Fostering an attitude of gratitude can profoundly impact your perspective and performance as a flight attendant. Reflect on the importance of recognizing the positives in your daily experiences and how this can enhance your service.

Personal Application:

Start a daily gratitude journal, noting three things you are thankful for at the end of each flight. These could be simple moments that brought you joy or connections you made with passengers.

Prayer: Heavenly Father, help me to foster an attitude of gratitude in my life and work. May I always recognize and appreciate the blessings around me, enriching my service and those I encounter.

Day 94: The Role of Initiative

Quote: *"Taking initiative enhances the travel experience."*

Scripture: "Whatever your hand finds to do, do it with all your might." -Ecclesiastes 9:10

Reflection: Your willingness to take initiative can lead to improved service and passenger experiences. Reflect on how being proactive in your role makes a positive difference.

Personal Application:

Identify an area where you can take initiative on your next flight, whether it's helping with a difficult task, suggesting improvements, or simply anticipating passenger needs.

_____

_____

_____

_____

_____

_____

_____

_____

_____

_____

Prayer: Lord, help me to recognize opportunities to take initiative. May I serve with purpose and enthusiasm, enhancing the experiences of all who travel with us.

Day 95: Building a Culture of Support

Quote: *"A supportive environment boosts morale and efficiency."*

Scripture: "Let us consider how we may spur one another on toward love and good deeds." - Hebrews 10:24

Reflection: Fostering a supportive work environment among your crew promotes camaraderie and teamwork. Reflect on how your encouragement and support can uplift your colleagues and enhance their performance.

Personal Application:

Reach out to a teammate to offer support or encouragement. This could be as simple as a compliment or asking how you could help them with their tasks.

Prayer: Heavenly Father, help me to foster a culture of support among my colleagues. May my actions encourage unity and positivity, improving our service and strengthening our team.

Day 96: The Importance of Self-Reflection

Quote: "Self-reflection fosters growth and improvement."

Scripture: "Examine yourselves to see whether you are in the faith; test yourselves." -2 Corinthians 13:5

Reflection: Regular self-reflection allows you to assess your actions, motivations, and areas for improvement. Reflect on how taking time to introspect enhances your service and personal development.

Personal Application:

Dedicate time at the end of each week to reflect on your service experiences. Write about what went well, what challenges you faced, and how you can grow moving forward.

_____

_____

_____

_____

_____

_____

_____

_____

_____

_____

Prayer: Lord, guide me in my practice of self-reflection. Help me to learn from my experiences and to continue growing in my service and character.

Day 97: The Impact of Professionalism

Quote: *"Professionalism enhances the overall flying experience."*

Scripture: "Whatever you do, do it all for the glory of God." -1 Corinthians 10:31

Reflection: Demonstrating professionalism in your role as a flight attendant sets the standard for quality service. Reflect on how your professionalism influences passengers' perceptions and experiences.

Personal Application:

Identify one aspect of your service where you can enhance your professionalism, whether it's improving your attire, communication, or knowledge about the aircraft and emergency procedures.

_____

_____

_____

_____

_____

_____

_____

_____

_____

_____

Prayer: Heavenly Father, help me to uphold a high standard of professionalism in my work. May my commitment to excellence reflect Your glory and inspire confidence in those I serve.

Day 98: The Role of Compassion

Quote: *"Compassion elevates service to a personal touch."*

Scripture: "Compassionate hearts, kindness, humility, meekness, and patience." -Colossians 3:12

Reflection: Embracing compassion allows you to connect with passengers more deeply, creating a memorable experience. Reflect on how showing compassion can alleviate anxiety and bring comfort to travelers.

Personal Application:

During your next flight, look for opportunities to express compassion to others, whether it's offering assistance, actively listening to concerns, or simply being present with a warm demeanor.

_____

_____

_____

_____

_____

_____

_____

_____

_____

_____

_____

Prayer: Lord, instill in me a spirit of compassion. May my interactions reflect Your love and understanding, creating a nurturing atmosphere for everyone on board.

Day 99: The Gift of Rest

Quote: *"Taking time to rest is vital for overall well-being."*

Scripture: "Come to me, all you who are weary and burdened, and I will give you rest." - Matthew 11:28

Reflection: Rest is essential to maintaining your physical and mental health as a flight attendant. Reflect on how prioritizing rest allows you to serve more effectively and joyfully.

Personal Application:

Schedule specific times for rest and relaxation this week. This could include getting enough sleep, engaging in hobbies, or taking time to unwind after a busy flight.

Prayer: Heavenly Father, remind me of the importance of rest in my life. Help me to prioritize my well-being, so I can serve with renewed energy and positive spirit.

Day 100: Celebrating the Journey

Quote: *"Celebrate the journey, for every step has shaped who you are becoming."*

Scripture: "This is the day that the Lord has made; let us rejoice and be glad in it." -Psalm 118:24

Reflection: Each flight presents opportunities for new experiences, connections, and personal growth. Reflect on how embracing this perspective can enhance your service and the overall atmosphere on board.

Personal Application:

Before your next flight, take a moment to acknowledge the unique experiences you anticipate. What excites you about today's journey? Write those thoughts down or share them with a teammate.

_____

_____

_____

_____

_____

_____

_____

_____

_____

_____

Prayer: Lord, thank You for the opportunity to embark on new adventures every day. Help me to embrace each flight with joy and a sense of purpose, creating memorable experiences for all those on board.

My Prayer of Salvation

Father God,

I am a sinner and need your forgiveness.

I believe that Jesus Christ shed His precious blood and died for my sin.

I am willing to change and turn from my sin.

I now invite Jesus Christ to come into my heart and life as my personal Lord and Savior.

DATE: _____

(This is your new "Birth Day")

Congratulations! You are now born again!

HALLELUJAH!!!

www.ingramcontent.com/pod-product-compliance
Lightning Source LLC
Chambersburg PA
CBHW050103170426
43198CB00014B/2438